Original title:

Under the Acacia

Copyright © 2025 Creative Arts Management OÜ

All rights reserved.

Author: Rory Fitzgerald

ISBN HARDBACK: 978-1-80566-649-3

ISBN PAPERBACK: 978-1-80566-934-0

Where Sky Meets the Leafy Realm

In a tree where the squirrels play,
A bird sings loud, come join the fray.
Nuts and seeds, a feast to share,
While raccoons plot with clever flair.

Beneath green canopies up high,
A froggy croaks, 'It's time to fly!'
But who's to leap, oh what a sight,
As bees cheer on their flying flight.

The Play of Light Through Verdant Space

Sunlight dances on the ground,
Tickling toes where joy is found.
A shadow hides, a game of peek,
With giggles soft, it's hide and seek.

Leaves wiggle, swaying to the tune,
While crickets chirp a cheeky ruin.
Laughter echoes, oh what a scene,
As ants march in their tiny team.

Solace Found Among the Fronds

Frogs in hats sip lemonade,
While butterflies join the parade.
Lizards basking in the fun,
Laugh at jokes from the rising sun.

Bunnies hop in their chic attire,
Playing tag, never will tire.
With friends so dear, it feels so right,
In this leafy land of pure delight.

The Breath of Nature in the Evening Light

As day dips low and shadows grow,
A party starts with a breezy flow.
Fireflies twinkle, stars above,
Nature's dance, all creatures love.

Crickets strum a lively beat,
While moonlit tales cannot be beat.
With every rustle, laughter spreads,
In this oasis where joy treads.

Richness of Roots that Ground Us

In a land of mischief, squirrels play,
Their acorns stolen, they shout hooray.
A dance-off starts, they wiggle and twirl,
Who knew they could spin like a funky swirl?

With roots intertwined, they'd form a pact,
To prank the owls, that's a solid fact.
They toss acorns high, no fear in sight,
Laughter erupts, as day turns to night.

Cascades of Color in the Breeze

Banners of leaves in a vibrant parade,
They flutter and flap, their dance is charade.
A butterfly sneezes, takes off, what a scene,
Comets of color, pure chaos between.

The flowers step out, dressed up in their best,
With bees on the mic, they're buzzing a jest.
A tulip trips over a daffodil's foot,
They laugh, till the sun dips, their humor is cute.

Fables that Rush with the River

Bubbly waters laughing, tales of surprise,
Fish wearing bowties with glittery eyes.
They gossip of frogs who wear hats made of reeds,
While crickets recite their own quirky deeds.

A turtle in glasses claims he's a sage,
While raccoons discuss the latest stage.
The river flows on, with twists and with turns,
A laughter-filled fable, as each creature learns.

Adrift in the Realm of Green Dreams

In the land where the grass tickles toes,
Dreams dance like shadows, where no one knows.
The dandelions giggle, they loft in the air,
As wishes are scattered without a care.

A rabbit named Flopsy, with tales so tall,
Claims he once out-ran a tree that could crawl.
In this realm of green, all worries take flight,
As humor blooms bright, turning wrongs into right.

A Place Where Dreams Take Root

In a shade where laughter grows,
We gather round with silly woes.
A squirrel steals snacks, oh what a thief,
We can't help but laugh, it's pure relief.

With dreams that sprout on leafy beams,
We craft our plans, ignite our schemes.
A picnic spreads, but ants arrive,
We squeal and dance, oh, we're alive!

Under skies where giggles dwell,
We spin our tales, we cast our spells.
A breeze that tickles, makes us squeal,
In this wonderland, we truly feel.

So come and join our merry crew,
With silly hats and skies so blue.
We'll share our laughs, our hopes, our dreams,
In this joyful place, nothing's as it seems.

Tales We Share Beneath Nature's Gaze

In the grove, where stories twine,
We trade our tales with fruity wine.
A bird mocks us, it has a flair,
We chuckle loud, we do not care.

The sun peeks through the boughs so green,
With every shade, a new routine.
A plump raccoon snags all our fries,
We're rolling on the grass, what a surprise!

We whisper secrets to the trees,
The leaves nod back, oh, what a tease!
With every breeze, a joke is told,
We laugh till sun fades into gold.

So gather round, let's cheer and sing,
In this bright world, let laughter ring.
With stories shared and silly grins,
In nature's arms, our fun begins.

Whispers Beneath the Branches

In the shade where laughter springs,
A squirrel juggles acorn rings,
The breeze whispers cheeky calls,
As raccoons plan their little brawls.

A chatter of birds, all in jest,
As they know they're simply the best,
A game of tag upon the breeze,
With giggles dancing through the trees.

Shadows of the Sunlit Grove

Beneath the sun's warm, winking eye,
A turtle spies a passing fly,
With a yawn and a lazy blink,
He dreams of snacks and a cool drink.

The shadows stretch, do a jig,
While a playful puppy finds a twig,
Chasing beams as they rapidly fall,
Trying hard not to trip at all.

Secrets Held by the Bark

The old tree holds secrets vast,
Of who played tag, and who fell fast,
Assorted tales through rings of time,
Of squirrels dressed as rocks in mime.

Beneath its arms, a picnic spreads,
With crumbs that dance around their heads,
A butterfly steals a sandwich bite,
While ants march in with all their might.

Dance of the Golden Leaves

Leaves twirl like dancers in a line,
Sipping dew from the morning shine,
A gust of wind shouts, 'What's the fuss?'
As acorns drop and giggles rush.

In frolicsome moves, they float and sway,
Spreading joy in their autumn ballet,
While little critters cheer the scene,
In the best little theater ever seen.

A Dreamscape Beneath Verdant Arches

Beneath leafy roofs, the squirrels conspire,
With acorns they hoard, their hearts full of fire.
The birds throw a party, each note a bold cheer,
While ants hold a meeting, all drinks are quite near.

A rabbit hops by, wearing socks that are polka,
He dances a jig, oh what a fine folka!
The shadows do giggle, the sunshine does clap,
As the wind joins the fun with a silly old flap.

The flowers are chatting, in colors so bright,
They gossip about bees who are bumbling in flight.
A funny old frog croaks, "What's the latest news?"
As tadpoles play tag in their tiny old shoes.

So join in the laughter, don't take life too serious,
For nature's a stage, and it's all quite curious.
With giggles and wiggles, let merriment start,
In this leafy enclave that warms every heart.

Lost in the Embrace of Nature

In a grove full of leaves where the sun likes to peek,
The squirrels are plotting some mischief all week.
They challenge the rabbits to a game of charades,
While the daisies roll over, folding their shades.

A butterfly winks, and the beetles declare,
"We're the real stars of this earthy affair!"
The worms sing their song from below with a twirl,
While the woodpecker dances, a bird in a whirl.

The trees crack their bark, sharing whispers so sly,
About the poor snail who tried flying—oh my!
He landed on grass with a soft little plop,
And now he will spend all day dreaming non-stop.

So let your heart giggle, let your spirit run wild,
For the great outdoors laughs, hugging us like a child.
With each rustle and murmur, find joy in the air,
In this merry embrace, you'll find love everywhere.

The Quietude of Solitude's Haven

In a corner of green where the bumblebees hum,
A flower tells secrets, "Oh, who's that? A plum?"
The petals erupt in laughter, their colors on show,
While the grass holds a competition; who can grow low?

A wise old tortoise thinks life's a fine race,
While watching the butterflies set a frenzied pace.
"I'll show them," he chuckles, "that slow can be fun!"
As he samples a leaf, "What a delightful run!"

A family of sheep play hopscotch with clouds,
While dandelions tumble, avoiding the crowds.
They gather for tea with a dash of bright zest,
As the sun dips its toes, giving night a warm jest.

So seek out this quiet where laughter runs free,
In the company of critters, you'll feel giddy glee.
For solitude's haven, with its playful embrace,
Is where giggles are shared, and joy finds its place.

The Language of Bark and Blossom

Listen closely, my friend, and you'll surely hear,
The trees share their jokes, full of giggles and cheer.
With roots in the ground, they laugh at their height,
While the sunbeams chuckle, "Oh, what a delight!"

The flowers are gossiping right next to the bugs,
"Did you see that old snail? He's in for some hugs!"
As the petals all flutter in breezy acclaim,
They debate who can dance—the wind joins the game.

A bee buzzes by, "I'm the cutest of all!"
Yet the dragonflies swoop with a dazzling sprawl.
The ladybugs chuckle and roll with the tide,
While the grasshoppers break into jazz with great pride.

In this silly world where laughter runs deep,
The language of nature is one that you keep.
So take in the humor, the joy of the trees,
In the chatter of flora, find fun on the breeze.

Serenity Amongst the Blossoms

In the shade where giggles bloom,
Bees debate on which flower's room.
Squirrels play hide and seek with cheer,
While ants march on, all wearing gear.

A frog croaks jokes from the nearby pond,
Lizards laugh at a curious blond.
Sunlight dances, a playful tease,
Even the flowers sway with ease.

A butterfly wears a dapper suit,
Claiming the title of fashion brute.
While petals toss their colors bright,
They whisper secrets, pure delight.

Nature's laughter fills the air,
With every rustling leaf laid bare.
In this charmed and silly scene,
Happiness reigns where grass is green.

A World Wrapped in Golden Hues

Beneath a canopy of sunny stare,
Gossipy bees buzz without a care.
A jester bird attempts to sing,
His off-key notes cause joy to spring.

Dancing shadows across the ground,
Sunbeams giggle, skipping around.
A caterpillar writes a pun,
'This is how we have our fun!'

The breeze tosses leaves in wild delight,
As chipmunks race from left to right.
Clouds chuckle, fluffing up the scene,
What a whimsical world, so serene!

In a place where laughter blooms bright,
Every critter is filled with delight.
Joy thrives where warmth does blend,
A cozy place where troubles end.

The Story of Leaves and Time

Leaves gossip like a pair of friends,
Telling tales that never end.
A breeze steals whispers from the tree,
Launching them like paper planes with glee.

Time slips by in a graceful swirl,
While acorns plot their next big whirl.
Each season throws a cheeky grin,
Noticing how the fun begins.

The sun takes selfies, capturing light,
As shadows play hide and seek in flight.
Nature jests, 'This isn't the end,
More stories await, just around the bend!'

When the twilight brings a soft sigh,
The tree awaits, watching the sky.
With laughter echoing far and wide,
Leaves fall, each one a delight-filled ride.

Conversations Held in Petal and Thorn

Petals whisper secrets loud,
While thorns wear grins, proud in their crowd.
A daisy quips, 'Life's a dream!'
While roses giggle, 'We're on the team!'

In this garden of friendly fights,
Every blossom shares their insights.
A cactus dances with a grumpy frown,
Turning thorns into a comedy gown.

The garden gnome pipes in with a joke,
'What's green and sings? Elvis Parsley.' He spoke.
With laughter weaving through each vine,
The flowers bloom, feeling divine.

In every petal, humor thrives,
A quirky mix of nature's lives.
So join the chat, don't be forlorn,
In this realm of petal and thorn!

Hues of Dusk and Dawn

In the glow of the evening light,
A squirrel dons a wig so bright.
He prances, twirls, and gives a wink,
While everyone stops to sip and think.

The sun slips down, a lazy thief,
As birds chirp songs of sheer belief.
A cat joins in, with gusto and flair,
Pretending not to see the stare.

With whispers soft, the colors blend,
As laughter echoes, never to end.
A dance parade with all the critters,
Where even the moon smirks and flitters.

As evening wraps around the day,
The stars appear, in a cheeky play.
They glow and giggle high above,
While dreams take flight, like a dove.

Tales of the Forgotten Roots

Long ago, when time was meek,
A worm wore glasses, quite unique.
He told grand tales of sun and rain,
While everyone laughed, despite the pain.

Beneath the soil, the stories grew,
With every giggle, the roots they flew.
A beetle dressed as a shady ghost,
Scared the ants, but they loved him most.

With tales of giants and tiny bees,
They cracked up at the talking trees.
Each story told with style and grace,
Life is a comedy, in this place.

The sun peeked down, with a curious eye,
As echoes of laughter filled the sky.
An orchestra of humor, sprouting seeds,
In the garden of fun, where laughter leads.

Songs of the Whispering Tree

In the breeze, a tree sings low,
With roots and branches, putting on a show.
Each leaf is a note, plucked with care,
While a raccoon dances, without a care.

The tree tells secrets, oh so spry,
Of a bird that thought it could fly high.
But missed the branch by just a tad,
And landed softly, feeling quite mad.

With rustling leaves, and laughter clear,
The heart of nature sings, my dear.
Snakes binding together, like a duo band,
While bees tap toes on the hot, dry sand.

In this cheerful grove, no frown to be found,
Just giggles and wiggles all around.
The songs of the tree, both silly and sweet,
Make every moment a joyful treat.

Petals in the Morning Dew

As dawn awakes with sparkling lights,
The flowers giggle in their tights.
A butterfly flutters, with spots of glee,
And shimmies along, just to be free.

Dewdrops dance on petals, they sway,
While a sneaky snail joins the fray.
He slips and slides, a slick little chap,
Making all the daisies take a nap.

A chorus of bees hums a tune,
While a frog croaks underneath the moon.
They spin a yarn of morning bliss,
Where nothing feels amiss, in this twist.

With laughter echoing in the air,
The garden blooms with love and care.
In every droplet, joy renews,
As petals soak in morning's hues.

Journeys Through the Green Canopy

Beneath the leaves, I seek my snack,
A squirrel scolds me, "Hey! Get back!"
I trip on roots, my dance is bold,
Nature's giggles, forever told.

With branches swaying, trees start to laugh,
Their whispers jumbled, like a silly gaffe.
A bird swoops down, steals my hat,
"Hey, that's not yours!" I shout with a spat.

A raccoon joins in, adds to the fray,
With a cheeky grin, he steals my bouquet.
The sunlight twinkles, a flickering tease,
As I chase critters with quirky decrees.

And as I stroll beneath this show,
I can't help but smile, let mischief flow.
In this green haven, such joy abounds,
Where laughter in leaves is the best of sounds.

Reflections of a Starlit Path

At twilight's veil, shadows play tricks,
I trip on stones, oh what a mix!
Under the moon's mischievous beam,
I stumble ahead, lost in a dream.

The nightingale sings, but oh, what a croak,
A frog jumps by, as if it's a joke.
I laugh at the creatures, all out of line,
This nightly circus, oh how divine!

Stars flicker and twirl, they wink and they sway,
I bow to the cosmos, then trip on my way.
The owls all hoot, they join in the fun,
In this merry moment, we're all truly one.

So under the sky, I dance with a grin,
Embracing these blunders, oh where do I begin?
Each stumble a story, each laugh a delight,
In the giggling darkness, everything feels right.

Harmony in Nature's Choir

In the meadow, voices rise and prance,
A rhythm of chaos, a wobbly dance.
The bees buzz off-key, what a strange hum,
While frogs play the drums, it's a nature's strum.

Leaves rustle softly, adding a beat,
While squirrels provide the tap of their feet.
A raccoon on stage, with a well-planned act,
Stealing the spotlight, heck, that's a fact!

The flowers, they sway, trying to find tune,
As a lonely snail warms up with a croon.
I join the performance, not shy in the pack,
With giggles and wiggles, I'll never hold back.

In this jolly concert, I lose all my cares,
With laughter and songs swirling in the air.
The night ends in giggles, oh what a cheer,
In nature's own choir, I feel so near.

The Call of the Earthbound Spirits

In the twilight hour, spirits arise,
With a tickle of tinsel and sparkle in their eyes.
They call out softly, "Come dance and twirl!"
But first, I trip, and give it a whirl!

Goblins with giggles pull me along,
While I stumble and fumble, I sing a wrong song.
"Your feet are wild!" they tease with flair,
I wink back and say, "It's just my hair!"

A wisp swirls by, makes fun of my shoes,
"Oh dear, you'll trip! Better pick up the blues!"
But I wag my finger, laughing it off,
And the earthbound spirits just cannot scoff.

In this joyous dance, shadows collide,
Each twist and turn invites a wild ride.
With laughter and mischief, I run with delight,
For in this magic place, the world feels just right.

Echoes of an Ancient Roots

In shadows deep, the laughs take flight,
Where squirrels dance in morning light,
A wisdom tree, with leaves so green,
Teaches us all to avoid the beans.

Its branches wave, a playful tease,
While ants march on with endless ease,
A gathering place for chattering fools,
Claiming the spot as their leafy schools.

Silent whispers crack the air,
Like secrets shared with those who dare,
Beneath the limbs, a jester's den,
Where cats conspire with their best friends.

And so we sit, with snacks in tow,
Under the branches, giggles flow,
For laughter rings in nature's halls,
Where ancient roots hold countless brawls.

Sunlight Flickers Through the Foliage

The sunlight plays a game of peek,
With shadows dancing through the week,
Sunbeams plot with a cheerful grin,
While lizards lounge and bask in sin.

The leaves, they chuckle, rustling loud,
Creating shade for the sleepy crowd,
Beneath this cover, mischief brews,
As bees and bugs swap funny news.

A picnic spread brings goofy sights,
With sandwiches that take to flight,
The ketchup bottle tries to run,
While ants host parties, oh what fun!

A ball rolls in, a daring quest,
For fragile friendships put to test,
But laughter reigns, a joyous scene,
In nature's light, where all's serene.

Birds of a Feather, singing Softly

A ruckus forms in the lofty trees,
As feathered friends share silly tease,
With tiny beaks and chatter bright,
They gossip 'bout leaves and worms at night.

Their tunes are quirky, a comical choir,
As they croon about their heart's desire,
A waltz on branches, oh so sweet,
While one bird tries to dance to a beat.

And here comes the crow with a swagger bold,
Reporting tales of shiny gold,
While pigeons puff up, chests out wide,
Debating who deserves to glide.

A feathery drama unfolds above,
In the embrace of nature's love,
For every chirp is packed with glee,
An avian tale for all to see.

A Symphony of Rustling Leaves

In melodies made by rustling sounds,
The leaves conspire on merry rounds,
A symphony of whimsical waves,
Creating a score that mischief craves.

The breezy fingers play their part,
As branches sway with all their heart,
While critters join, percussion fits,
Making music from the forest's wits.

A rhythmic dance, a jolt of breeze,
As sounds collide with playful ease,
The bushes hum in laughter's tune,
While shadows play beneath the moon.

So join the fun, let voices rise,
In nature's chorus that never dies,
For every hush, and every cheer,
Adds to the charm that we all hear.

Starlit Nights in the Garden

At midnight, frogs begin their tune,
While owls hoot like they're at a swoon.
The fireflies dance with glowing grace,
As my cat chases shadows, losing the race.

Chairs recline on the soft, cool grass,
My drink spills where the beetles pass.
Stars twinkle like they've lost the plot,
A secret show that's quite the spot!

Dreams Among the Blossoming Foliage

In a tent of leaves, I laid down my head,
Dreams of sandwiches and chocolate spread.
Bees buzz past with a gossip to share,
While squirrels debate on who's got the flair.

A brave little worm, he peeks out his door,
Wonders if he can dance on the floor.
But a bird flies by, and he dives for a hole,
Dreams of grand parties are suddenly stole!

A Symphony of Thorns and Petals

Petals scatter, a colorful mess,
Thorns say, 'Careful!' with a prickly stress.
A bumblebee hums a tune so sweet,
While ants march by with no time for defeat.

In this orchestra, chaos has reign,
With a trumpet of frogs, it's hard to explain.
As I sip lemonade, a bee lands with flair,
Then takes a dive—oops! Right in my hair!

The Serenity of Shade

A hammock swings, a gentle sway,
As the sun burns bright, I find my way.
A lizard lounges, bold and spry,
While I dream of tacos drifting by.

Suddenly a breeze tickles my feet,
The cat glares, thinks that's quite a treat.
With laughter nearby, kids run around,
I raise my glass, and we chill without sound.

Revelations in the Twilight Glow

In the dusk, with a snap and crack,
A squirrel debates if it's time for a snack.
With acorns piled high like a small tower,
He's got dinner plans that might take an hour.

A bird on a branch sings a tune so bright,
While a cat creeps up, all ready for a bite.
The bird shouts, "Not today, you silly old prude!"
And flaps away, leaving the cat in a mood.

A breeze flutters by, whispering cheeky tales,
Of frogs in tuxedos and silly snails.
They dance in their shells with great jubilation,
As twilight descends on their wild celebration.

It's a party of laughter, a comedy spree,
Where nature's the stage, and the audience is free.
So grab your popcorn, come join the show,
In the enchanting glow of the twilight show.

Beneath the Swaying Boughs

A rabbit hops in with a curious stare,
Claiming the spot while the crowd's unaware.
He's put on a hat that's far too too big,
And struts like a king, doing a silly jig.

The owl on the limb rolls its big wise eyes,
At the rabbit's pure chaos, oh what a surprise!
"Who invited the clown?" the owl tries to say,
But the rabbit just dances, come what may.

A toddler climbs up, full of giggles and grins,
As the branches below shake, the laughter begins.
With laughter so loud that the breezes get shy,
Even the rocks seem to chuckle nearby.

Nature's a theater, where humor takes flight,
Watch as the creatures put on a delight.
Every critter has roles, each in perfect place,
In a comical world where smiles take space.

A Haven for the Wandering Soul

A wayward leaf whirls in a hiccuping dance,
While ants hold a conga, taking a chance.
They march with a beat, tiny feet in a row,
Making music from crumbs, oh the show must go!

A chubby old toad is the bouncer tonight,
Keeping order and chuckling at every slight.
"Step right up, join the jamboree,
The fun's getting wild, just wait and see!"

A duck with a quack that echoes like song,
Is asking the fireflies to come join along.
They twinkle and giggle, igniting the scene,
As the night comes alive, it's a sight to be seen!

Frogs leap and frogs croak, it's a riotous blaze,
Echoes of laughter set the forest ablaze.
Every creature a friend in this raucous delight,
In a haven of laughter that sparkles so bright.

The Melody of Nature's Heartbeat

A mouse with a flute thinks it's ready to play,
But the notes come out funny, in a wobbly way.
With each little squeak, he holds his ground proud,
And the other critters gather, all forming a crowd.

A fox in the back rolls its eyes with a grin,
"Is that music or just where the mischief begins?"
But soon everyone's clapping, their paws keeping beat,
To the mouse's wild tune, it's an odd little feat.

The wind adds a whistle, the leaves start to sway,
As critters all join in this sweet disarray.
From crickets to owls, all give it a try,
It's a raucous ensemble that tickles the sky.

So join in the fun, find your rhythm in jest,
Nature's a stage where the laughter's the best.
With melodies draping the night like a quilt,
In a symphony made by the joy that we built.

Gentle Breezes Through the Lattice

A squirrel in a bowler hat,
Waltzes round, so fine and spry.
Among the blooms he chats away,
As bees all buzz and flutter by.

The tickling wind whispers jokes,
To flowers dressed in bright array.
They giggle as they sway and bend,
While ants plan their parade today.

A butterfly in shades of blue,
Twirls and dives with eerie grace.
As daisies laugh, they shout, "Hooray!"
And dance in blissful, bright embrace.

The sun peeks through a leafy frame,
And smiles at creatures wild and free.
The world is full of silly fun,
In this wacky, green jubilee.

Guardians of the Verdant Realm

A raccoon wears a crown of leaves,
Declaring, "I'm your noble king!"
His subjects bow, and some just sneeze,
While crickets hear the laughter ring.

A turtle dons a cap of grass,
Proclaiming, "I will take my time!"
He plods along, while near him, fast,
A rabbit hops with cheeky rhyme.

The owls hoot tales of great delight,
As shadows dance beneath a tree.
With every dusk, they weave a night,
That echoes with ridiculous glee.

In this realm of green and cheer,
The guardians wear silly grins,
In laughter's mist, we shed our fear,
And join the dance—the joy begins!

Memories in the Dappled Light

A lizard wearing shoes too big,
Skids and slides across the ground.
With every leap, he sings a jig,
His silly antics do astound.

The shadows play peek-a-boo with sun,
As little critters burst with glee.
The sound of laughter has begun,
In dappled light, they're wild and free.

A snail with shades that gleam so bright,
Claims he's the fastest, oh, so grand!
But while he's bragging in the light,
A tortoise strolls—he's got it planned.

The day drifts on in playful bliss,
With memories that tickle the mind.
In every corner, there's sweet happiness,
Nature's jesters, oh, so kind.

Nature's Embrace in the Stillness

A frog in a top hat holds a show,
With dance moves that are quite absurd.
The crickets cheer, they want to know
His secret—does he sing or curd?

A breeze brings whispers, soft and light,
As flowers sway in gentle tease.
"Who's the king of dance tonight?"
The field rejoices, lost in ease.

The clouds parade in fluffy hats,
While whispers fill the air with cheer.
The sun joins in, with sprinkles and sprats,
As nature winks, a hug so near.

In stillness found, the laughter flows,
It dances through the vibrant green.
Together we find joy that grows,
In every moment, pure and keen.

Surrendering to the Forest's Quiet

In the hush of the trees, I take a nap,
Snoring like a bear, what a wild trap!
The squirrels hold a council, planning a heist,
While I'm dreaming of peanut butter on toast, it's nice!

A bird starts to giggle, I blink my eyes,
Turns out I'm the joke, what a surprise!
They all point their wings, chattering loud,
In the kingdom of leaves, I sleep like a crowd!

Green whispers and chuckles fill the space,
Nature's own stand-up, a leafy embrace.
Laughter in shades of green all around,
I can't help but join in without making a sound!

As the sun dips low, shadows become long,
The forest sings softly, a quirk in the song.
I surrender in giggles, 'till day ends its race,
Knocked out by the humor of this leafy place!

Songs of Stillness and Gentle Sway

Twisting branches sway, like they're doing a dance,
They tease the small critters, giving them a chance.
Bumblebees buzzing, discussing their plans,
While I join in, swaying, inspired by their stance!

The wind joins the chorus, a playful refrain,
Tickling my nose, making me feel quite insane.
As I stand in the sunlight, my shadows conspire,
They wiggle and jiggle, sparking laughter like fire!

A raccoon pops his head out, giving a stare,
As if he's judging my dance without a care.
But who's really watching? Is it him or the trees?
In a forest of mischief, it's quite hard to tease!

Spinning and twirling, I'm lost in delight,
With a whirl of the breeze, I take off in flight.
Zero grace in my rhythm, but laughter's my friend,
In the songs of stillness, on laughter, I'll depend!

Enchantment Beneath Twinkling Stars

Midnight brings giggles, as the stars start to peek,
Their twinkle's a wink, a real cosmic cheek!
The trees start to chuckle, their leaves all aglow,
Whispering secrets that only they know.

A fox does a twirl, in moonlight's soft glow,
He thinks he's a dancer, puts on quite a show!
I clap for his brilliance, though he trips on a root,
In the moonlit arena, he's quite the cute brute!

Fireflies sparkle, like tiny disco balls,
They light up the night, answering my calls.
With a jig and a giggle, I join the parade,
In this silly nocturne, no plans need to fade!

The owl lets out laughter, deep and profound,
Echoing through branches, a wise, quirky sound.
In the night's grand performance, I play my small part,
With joy in my spirit and a dance in my heart!

Embraced by the Green Empress

The green lady beckons with a humorous grin,
She wraps me in vines, like I'm wearing a tin!
Her branches are tickling, a playful embrace,
Taking me captive, in this leafy place!

I stand here, bemused, a leaf on my hat,
A crown from the forest, how about that?
The frogs serenade me with songs full of glee,
As I laugh through the ferns, just as wild as can be!

Her laughter is wild, the wind at her side,
Dancing through trunks, like a joyful ride.
And as I trip lightly on this soft forest floor,
I'm caught in her magic, who could ask for more?

With roots intertwining, she pulls me in close,
In the arms of the green, I become her proud host.
Together we giggle at the antics of fate,
In splendor and humor, it's never too late!

The Call of the Sunlit Boughs

Birds plotting in the leaves,
Chasing dreams of crumbly treats,
Lively shadows dance and weave,
As sunlight plays on tiny feet.

Squirrels wear their acorn hats,
Boasting tales of nutty finds,
While a curious cat chats,
In a language that binds.

Laughter echoes, soft and sweet,
As branches whisper silly songs,
Inviting all to take a seat,
In a world where no one belongs.

A breeze brings tickles from the trees,
Leaves giggle as they sway with ease,

A Tapestry of Light and Shadow

Dappled spots upon the grass,
Where mischief finds its perfect stage,
Each critter slips, each acorn has,
Its own tale of a funny rage.

The sunbeams play a game of peek,
As ants parade in straight lines bold,
While a lazy lizard, oh so sleek,
Basks in warmth, feeling uncontrolled.

A butterfly, all dressed in gold,
Challenges a spider's web,
Both boast a story to be told,
In the dance of late-day ebb.

Laughter mingles with the dusk,
As shadows stretch beyond their bounds.

The Soft Murmur of Nature's Heart

A frog croaks like a broken bell,
As rabbits giggle, hopping by,
The grasses sway and say, "Oh well!"
While crickets chirp a lullaby.

Bumblebees buzz with much delight,
They juggle pollen like a sport,
While bugs in twos prepare for flight,
In this nature's nightly court.

The gentle wind, a playful tease,
Giggles through the flowers' hue,
And whispered tales in evening breeze,
Promise mischief yet to pursue.

The moon peeks down, a silver coin,
To catch the laughter on the lawn.

Rustling Thoughts in the Evening Breeze

A rustle in the grass at dusk,
As critters plot and scheme away,
Their twinkling eyes, quite full of brusque,
Share secrets of the waning day.

A hedgehog rolls, a ball of glee,
While shadows dance upon the ground,
And whispers float like honeyed tea,
Spilling laughter all around.

The nightingale, with comfy hum,
Sings songs of funny little woes,
While fireflies flash, all bright and dumb,
Like twinkling stars in nature's prose.

Amidst the fun, a world transformed,
As night reveals its lighter side.

Contemplations in the Shade

A squirrel did jest, in a curious mood,
He danced 'round a shadow, as though it were food.
A bird chimed in, with a quip quite absurd,
'This tree is a palace, or haven, or herd!'

With leaves like confetti, they plotted a feast,
On acorns and laughter, they'd munch like a beast.
The breeze carried giggles, a hilarious cheer,
As bees joined the party and sipped on the beer.

In the dappled delight, time seemed to pause,
A rabbit in costume, wearing a faux-claws.
Each shade brought a chuckle, each flicker a grin,
While ants held a meeting, debating on sin!

Oh joy in the flicker, where shadows do play,
Nature's own jesters, amusing each day.
The world spun around, yet here it stood still,
In fun-filled communion, atop nature's hill.

Beneath the Velvet Canopy

A lizard lounged lazy, with style on display,
It wore shades of leather, and striped polka play.
A rabbit declared, 'This is far too chic!'
In fashion faux pas, they all shared a peek.

The wind whispered secrets, in breezy delight,
As squirrels organized fashion shows, just for spite.
Zebras on stilts pranced, with cotton candy hair,
While bees cheered their efforts with honey to spare.

Every fern had a giggle, each trunk had a quirk,
As worms told tall tales, with bravado and smirk.
The laughter rang loud in the shimmering sun,
While critters contested on who's having fun.

With a wink and a nudge, in the soft, dappled glow,
Joy found its way; like a whimsical show.
Life's quirkiest circus, under leaves—oh so grand,
In the velvet embrace of this whimsical land.

Whispers Beneath the Canopy

What's that I hear? A chortle, a cheer?
A platypus practices, 'Can you hear me, dear?'
With feathers on head, and a bowtie quite bold,
He thinks he's a king, so the tales all are told.

A frog in a top hat, with a cane made of vine,
Proclaimed with a leap, 'I'm the best! Yes, divine!'
While turtles debated on who'd yodel best,
They laughed till they fell, like a real comedy fest.

The shadows were chatty, with gossip in tow,
While mice drew caricatures, putting on a show.
A parade of the zany under branches of green,
Where each little nook held a comedy scene.

As whispers collided, in the sweet scented air,
The trees held their sides, in the joy they would share.
With humor as rich as the roots that entwine,
They danced on a line where the funny meets spry.

Shadows of the Golden Tree

A chicken declared it, the best spot in town,
With dreams of egg muffins, she strutted around.
The crow puffed up proudly, with tales that he'd weave,
Of mischief and mayhem that none would believe!

A tap on the bark called a laughter parade,
As fireflies gathered, ready to raid.
With glow sticks of magic in bright, buzzing flares,
They lit up the night, leading dance through the airs.

A snail made a statement, 'I'm slower than most,'
But winked with a grin, like a cheeky host.
Each shadow a muse, with a tickle of fun,
As critters united, their laughter just spun.

In the space where the day fades to silky dreams,
The golden tree shimmers, with giggles and schemes.
In the heart of the night, wild mischief takes flight,
As shadows grow tall, brightening up every sight.

Secrets in the Treetop Breeze

In the high branches, a squirrel speaks,
Nuts are his treasures, not for the weak.
He hoards in silence, with careful glee,
While birds gossip sweetly, like gossiping bees.

The wind tickles leaves, they start to sway,
A lazy lizard joins the fun today.
He lounges on branches, a king on his throne,
Claiming the sunlight, all warmth of his own.

A parrot squawks in a ridiculous tone,
Repeating the secrets he's shamelessly known.
While ants march below with snacks for the feast,
Their tiny parade is a sight, not the least.

With laughter and chatter, the canopies sing,
All critters unite to enjoy their bling.
So when you walk by, take a moment to see,
The hilarity hidden in this grand marquee.

Dancing with the Desert Sun

In the blazing heat, a cactus prances,
Dressed in green, it takes joyful chances.
With arms all outstretched, it sways side to side,
Bowing to shadows where funny things hide.

A lizard with flair, in sequined attire,
Struts down the rocks, his moves never tire.
He twirls 'round a stone, showing off his tail,
While crickets beat rhythms that never go pale.

Juggling some flies with an amazing skill,
A toad starts to hop, it's his dream to fulfill.
And the sun laughs and burns, but they dance with delight,

Creating a show that gets better at night.

With each vibrant step under golden rays,
The creatures unite in their whimsical ways.
So join in the revel, leave worries behind,
In the desert's embrace, hilarious fun you'll find.

Beneath the Sprawling Branches

A bear with a hat enjoys afternoon tea,
Sipping on honey, as happy as can be.
While hedgehogs spin tales of bravery grand,
With dramatic gestures and paws that command.

A rabbit in shades tells jokes on a whim,
Half the crowd snickers, the other half's grim.
Yet laughter erupts, it's a rollicking sight,
When the punchline lands, they all leap in fright.

A sly fox in sneakers conducts a grand show,
With dancing and prancing, he steals the spotlight glow.
Though clumsy he trips, on his own two big feet,
The audience roars — what a hilarious feat!

With moments like these beneath leafy domes,
Funny friends gather, creating their homes.
So if you feel dull, just wander and roam,
To laugh in the branches, you'll always feel home.

The Embrace of Leaf and Sky

Two raccoons, quite crafty, craft shadows and schemes,
While dreaming of snacks and their sweet night-time dreams.
They plan a grand heist of the shiny new trash,
And giggle together, as neighbors all splash.

The wind carries whispers of bear and his plans,
To dance on the lawn with his pals in big bands.
But balancing antics cause quite the ordeal,
As he stumbles and tumbles, oh what a big deal!

Polly the parrot, with a laugh that is loud,
Excitedly squawks, drawing quite the big crowd.
She tells of the mischief the bats had last night,
All swooping and diving, oh what a swift sight!

So come join the revelry, laugh 'til you cry,
For nothing compares with the fun in the sky.
In moments so joyful, with friends ever near,
The magic persists, let's all spread the cheer!

Swaying to Nature's Rhythm

In the breeze the leaves do dance,
A squirrel takes a daring chance.
With acorn hat and tiny feet,
He wobbles on, oh what a feat!

The sunbeams play a game of tag,
While butterflies do twirl and wag.
A laughter echoes through the trees,
As nature hums and shakes its knees!

The grass joins in on this delight,
A jig that lasts from day to night.
The choir sings, both loud and clear,
"What a party! Come join us here!"

So take a breath and share a grin,
Let nature's fun just draw you in.
With every sway and happy tune,
The woods become a grand festoon!

The Heartbeat of Ancient Woods

In the realm where trees unite,
The owls play hide and seek by night.
A fox struts by in dapper style,
With a wink that makes the whole woods smile.

The mushrooms grumble, quite a sight,
"Please don't step on us, that's not polite!"
While rabbits hop, quite full of sass,
With bouncy tails that wiggle past.

A wise old tortoise cracks a joke,
"Don't rush, dear friends, or you'll just choke!"
The trees all nod and shift their leaves,
Laughter echoes in the eaves!

So join the dance, let spirits soar,
In ancient woods, there's always more.
With every laugh and every cheer,
You'll find that magic lingers near!

Beneath the Canopy's Arc

The branches sway, a playful tease,
As squirrels plot to steal some cheese.
A bird on high sings off-key tunes,
While ants march proud in tiny prunes.

The shadows giggle, playing tricks,
As beetles don their little kicks.
A lizard takes a sunlit pose,
While a grumpy snail grumbles and doze.

The grasshoppers leap with a loud cheer,
"Let's start a band, we've got no fear!"
Frogs croak loud their froggy rap,
While fireflies light up with a clap.

So gather 'round, dear friends of mine,
In the arc of leaves, let joy align.
With silly songs and giddy play,
Nature's laughter brightens the day!

A Tapestry of Nature's Colors

The flowers bloom in every hue,
While bugs break out in waltzes too.
A ladybug spins round and round,
Creating joy where it's abound.

With petals soft and scents so sweet,
A dandelion's on its feet.
"It's time to float, I'll catch a breeze!"
And off it goes with such great ease!

The colors swirl, a vibrant show,
A kaleidoscope in sun's warm glow.
When butterflies join in the dance,
Even the daisies start to prance!

So come and paint your day anew,
In nature's canvas, bright and true.
With every shade and joyful sound,
A tapestry of joy is found!

The Shade of Forgotten Dreams

In shadows where we used to hide,
The squirrels play with dreams denied.
The sunbeams dance, a silly prank,
As we debate which fruit is drank.

A picnic spread, a wild charade,
With sandwiches that seem homemade.
The ants invade, a tiny crew,
Marching to steal our lunch and stew.

An ice cream cone, a sticky mess,
Drips to the ground, oh what a stress!
We laugh aloud, our worries gone,
As laughter bounces on the lawn.

And in this shade, where tales conspire,
We craft tall tales that never tire.
The laughter echoes, bright and bold,
In tales of squirrels that steal our gold.

Where the Wildflowers Bloom

In fields where wild things seem to play,
I found my socks—a fleeting stay.
Worn by the breeze, in patterns neat,
The flowers chuckle at my feet.

Butterflies swirl in bright ballet,
While bees proclaim their busy sway.
They bump and buzz, a comic scene,
As if they're part of a grand routine.

A dandelion's mischievous grin,
Springs up like pop-up jokes within.
And I can't help but bend to tease,
A wishful whisper rides the breeze.

So here I sit, with grass-stained knees,
Sharing secrets with the trees.
We gossip 'bout the sun's bright tune,
Where laughter lingers 'neath the moon.

Memories in the Rustling Grass

The grass has stories, tall and grand,
Of secret meetings, a small band.
We played tag with shadows in the light,
While giggles echoed, pure delight.

The wind whispers tales that we once spun,
Of treasure maps and how we'd run.
With ketchup stains and chip crumbs shared,
Our little kingdom, we declared.

And as we fell on laughter's sighs,
The daisies peeked with curious eyes.
We declared ourselves the kings of fun,
While clouds above just rolled and spun.

Each tuft of grass a tale to tell,
Of summer days that cast a spell.
With dreams afloat, we danced and sang,
In memories rustling, where joy sprang.

The Tranquility of a Summer's Afternoon

A gentle breeze, a lazy tune,
The sun hangs high, a golden rune.
With lemonade and a grin so wide,
We lounge around, nowhere to hide.

The laughter drifts like cotton candy,
As someone plays the ukulele handy.
The birds chirp jokes, a feathery choir,
While ants perform their tiny tire.

A napkin flies, a wind mischief,
Chasing a dust cloud, oh what a riff!
We giggle at the chase's peak,
And settle down with ice cream streak.

In this sweet peace, no cares to find,
The sun sets soft, our hearts entwined.
We grin at dusk—the day's parade,
As memories brighten the serenade.

The Laughter of Children in the Shade

Beneath the branches wide and grand,
Kids giggle, play, and make a stand.
A game of tag with squeaky shoes,
Chasing dreams while shaking off blues.

With sticky fingers and goofy grins,
They spot the ants and debate their sins.
A worm is named and crowned a king,
While laughter echoes, oh what joy they bring!

The sun peeks through, a golden spy,
"Look! A cloud!" one shouts with a sigh.
But here they stay, with a giggle parade,
In this jolly realm, their small fortunes made.

And then it drizzles, oh what a fuss,
Kids spin and twirl, "Let's make a bus!"
In puddles deep, they bravely leap,
While laughter bubbles—it's time for sleep.

Savoring Sunbeams and Shadows

Sunbeams slink on grass so bright,
Like lazy cats in afternoon light.
Each shadow dances a comic jig,
While bees chase sunlight, oh so big!

The picnic ants have quite a feast,
Burgers gone? Not in the least!
They parade on crumbs, and what a sight,
Toasting to flavors, they laugh in delight.

A squirrel snickers at a nearby spread,
Thinking of peanuts—"Oh, they'll be fed!"
The kids scream, "No! That's our last bite!"
But the critter just rolls, its eyes filled with light.

In sunbeam realms, with giggles galore,
They trade silly games; who could ask for more?
When shadows grow long in the play's sweet end,
They're the lively jesters, the best of friends.

The Dance of Flora and Fauna

In a green ballet, leaves sway and twirl,
As bees and butterflies shimmer and whirl.
"Catch me if you can!" the ladybug says,
While daisies nod, cheering in a daze.

The flowers gossip about silly bees,
"Did you see that dive? Oh, what a tease!"
Sunflowers grin with their heads held high,
While lazy clouds drift on by.

A squirrel spins tales of nutty delight,
Of acorns stolen in the dead of night.
"Look! A feather!" calls the cheeky blue jay,
As flowers chuckle, "He's gone astray!"

Together they dance in the fading sun,
Creating ruckus—oh, what fun!
Beneath the giggles of nature's fair play,
Life is a jest on a bright, breezy day.

In the Realm of Gentle Breezes

Gentle breezes play tag with the leaves,
Whispers giggle through branches that tease.
A branch bows down, "Come play with me!"
As butterflies flutter, oh so free.

A ticklish grass tickles tiny toes,
The sun dips low, painting the rose.
Each laugh echoes, a child's glee,
Chasing giggles—come dance with me!

Rustling papers, notes of delight,
A paper airplane takes sudden flight.
"Look at it soar!" the children cheer,
While wind nudges, "I'm flying here!"

In this kingdom of whimsy, laughter reigns,
With treasures of joy, no room for pains.
As stars peek out, a fun night's embrace,
They've savored the sun—what a merry place!

Echoes of Laughter Under the Canopy

In the shade where shadows play,
A squirrel steals lunch, runs away.
The birds all gossip, tweet a tune,
While ants debate their afternoon.

Giggles bounce on a breeze so light,
As grasshoppers leap, taking flight.
A funny dance, one slips and falls,
Laughter echoes through leafy halls.

A raccoon joins the dance floor crowd,
Waving his paws, feeling so proud.
The breeze nudges a feathery friend,
Startling laughter, around the bend.

As he trips and tumbles away from the show,
We all chuckle, let the good vibes flow.
In this haven, munching, we bask,
What joy resides, just ask and you'll grasp.

Guardians of Secrets in Leafy Shadows

A wise old owl, perched on a limb,
Tells tales that make our hearts swim.
The shadows giggle, the leaves sway,
As secrets tiptoe, dance, and play.

A frog croaks loudly, claiming his throne,
While crickets chirp with a snarky tone.
Whispers float in the afternoon,
As spiders weave webs, crafting a tune.

The raccoon spies with a sneaky stare,
Calculating mischief in the warm air.
With a tug of his tail, he scuttles away,
Leaving behind smiles that won't decay.

In shadows deep, the laughter spills,
From secrets shared and thrill-filled chills.
Nature's jesters, all in a row,
As the sun dips low, we all steal the show.

The Warmth of a Whispered Promise

Beneath a bough, friends huddle tight,
Exchanging secrets, full of delight.
A breeze tickles leaves; it starts to mix,
With giggles and whispers, a wondrous fix.

A chipmunk knows just where to hide,
In laughter's glow, he takes great pride.
With peanuts stashed, he makes quite the scene,
A tiny thief—oh, how obscene!

Promises made in sunlight's gleam,
As silly stories float like a dream.
Each chuckle and grin, a bond that's sealed,
In nature's playground, joy is revealed.

With every laugh, the world feels bright,
In whispers soft, we share delight.
Our hearts all dance, with freedom's cheer,
In this lively riot, we hold dear.

Nature's Canvas in Golden Hues

As dusk wraps gold around the trees,
We paint the sky with laughter's ease.
A butterfly winks, all in a whirl,
Tickling daisies, making them twirl.

Mice chase shadows, quick on their toes,
While nature chuckles, and mischief grows.
With tiny capers and frolicsome glee,
Every creature joins the jamboree.

Sunlight tiptoes, casting its glow,
On friends who tumble, delight in tow.
Each giggle bounces on warm air's back,
In our vivid world, nothing we lack.

Painting a scene rich with cheer,
Each stroke of joy, perfectly clear.
In this moment, our spirits take flight,
Nature's canvas, oh what a sight!

www.ingramcontent.com/pod-product-compliance
Lightning Source LLC
Chambersburg PA
CBHW072134070526
44585CB00016B/1675